W9-CPX-252

Copyright © 2001, 1999, 2000 by Grolier Enterprises, Inc.
All rights reserved. Published by Grolier Incorporated, a subsidiary of Scholastic Inc.
Questions Kids Ask is a registered trademark of Grolier, Inc.

No part of this publication may be reproduced, or stored in a retrieval system, or transmitted in any form
or by any means, electronic, mechanical, photocopying, recording, or otherwise, without written permission
of the publisher. For information regarding permission, write to
Grolier Incorporated, Attention: Permissions Department,
90 Old Sherman Turnpike, Danbury, Connecticut 06816.

Library of Congress Cataloging-in-Publication Data available

ISBN 0-439-33717-8

10 9 8 7 6 5 4 3 2 1   01 02 03 04 05

Printed in the U.S.A.

First printing, October 2001

"Why do pigs roll in mud?"

...and other

Questions Kids Ask™

About Mammals Big & Small

📖 SCHOLASTIC

New York   Toronto   London   Auckland   Sydney
Mexico City   New Delhi   Hong Kong   Buenos Aires

TABLE OF CONTENTS

QUESTIONS KIDS ASK ABOUT MAMMALS BIG & SMALL

Dear QKA Reader,

I have a confession to make: Mammals are a mystery to me.

Take camels, for instance. What's the story with that hump? Elephants have huge ears and kangaroos have pouches, but why? (Lizards don't need any of that stuff. We're naturally beautiful!)

Why do skunks stink? Can groundhogs predict the weather? (I've never met a groundhog who was THAT smart!) And what is it about a red cloth that can make a bull so angry? (Sounds to me like someone needs to relax!)

You're a mammal, too, so maybe you know all the reasons mammals do the stuff they do! But just in case you don't, this book has the answers.

Read on! And keep on asking questions.

Your pondering pal,

Leonardo da Lizard

P.S. I need to get a closer look at some of these creatures. See if you can spy me on every page of this book as I conduct my research.

What is the largest creature that ever lived?

If you're thinking dinosaur, think again.

The blue whale takes first place for being the largest animal. It can be as long as 100 feet (31 m) and weigh as much as 200 tons (181 t)! By comparison, the biggest dinosaur weighed only 35 tons (32 t).

Blue whales have a big appetite, but what they eat is plankton, tiny plants and animals that float in the ocean, and krill, small shrimp-like creatures.

Whales are mammals. They breathe air, have hair, give birth, and nurse their babies until they are grown. These whales may be giants, but they're amazingly gentle.

8

EXTRA

Whales don't have vocal chords, but that doesn't stop them from singing. Their songs come from pushing air through channels and cavities inside their heads. Their tunes include clicks, whistles, and even humming noises.

Five Friends with Fins
Whales are found in every ocean.
Here are a few of the common types:

Orca   Sperm   Humpback   Gray   Minke

Quiet, leaf-eating giraffes are the world's tallest mammals. They wander the grassy plains of Africa in herds of 30 to 40, eating the leaves from spiky shrubs and trees. Acacia trees are one of their favorites.

Male giraffes tend to be a little taller than females. Some males grow to 18 or even 20 feet (5.5 to 6.1 m) long. The tallest females reach between 15 and 17 feet (4.6 and 5.2 m) tall. Males weigh between 1,765 and 4,255 pounds (800 and 1,930 kg); females reach between 1,215 and 2,600 pounds (550 and 1,180 kg).

Even though a giraffe's neck is extra-long, it contains only seven vertebrae, just like the necks of most other mammals. The hump on the giraffe's shoulders is the point where its powerful neck muscles connect to its body.

What is the tallest mammal?

It wins by a neck.

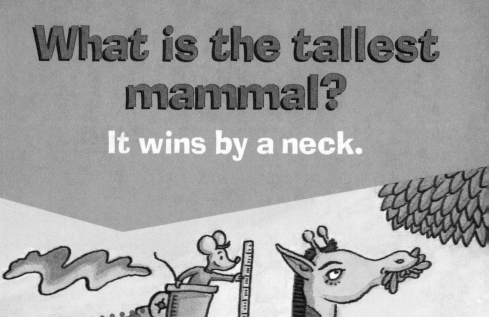

EXTRA

Giraffes are one of the few mammals to be born with horns. When a baby giraffe is born, its horns lie flat against its skull. They stand up about one week after birth.

Giraffe Facts

A giraffe's tongue is 18 to 20 inches (46 to 51 cm) long.
A giraffe's tail can be 3 feet (91 cm) long.
A giraffe's life span is about 25 years.

Do all mammals see color?

The answer isn't **black** and white.

Mammals' color vision depends on whether they are active during the day or night. Mammals that are active in the day, or diurnal, tend to be able to see color. Some diurnal mammals, such as human beings, have very good color vision. Others, such as dogs, have color vision that's more limited.

Mammals that are active at night, or nocturnal, usually don't have color vision. They don't really need it, though, because colors aren't very visible in the dark. Instead, nocturnal animals have eyes that are better at seeing fine shades of black, white, and gray.

EXTRA
Humans see colors well because of special cells called cones. We have three kinds of cones that let us see red, green, and blue light. Together, these cones help us see all the colors.

Do mammals change color?

Some mammals put on a new coat in winter.

EXTRA

The snowshoe hare earned its name because of its oversized hind feet. These specialized feet pack down the snow so that the hare can move more easily—the same way snowshoes work for people.

You're probably familiar with the way some mammals blend with their surroundings. A tiger's striped coat, for instance, provides perfect camouflage when the big cat is stalking prey in the high grass.

But if mammals are to blend in with surroundings that change, the animals must change as well. Arctic hares and snowshoe hares are perfect examples of mammals that change with the seasons.

Both species live in cold, northern climates. In summer, these regions are grassy and the soil is brown. In winter, their homes are covered with snow.

So the hares adapt. Their summer coats are brown, with hints of red and gray, to blend with the undergrowth. As the weather turns cold, the hares shed their summer coats and grow fluffy, white coats to blend with the snow in winter.

11

Why do dogs wag their tails?

Your pooch wants to tell you a thing or two.

A wagging tail is a dog's way of saying, "I'm happy!" It's like people greeting one another with smiles.

Dogs are social animals who want to be part of a group or a pack. Scientists say dogs even see their human owners as dogs. No wonder your dog keeps trying to share its feelings with you!

If your pooch's ears are folded back and its teeth are bared, you can be sure it is angry or defensive. If your dog's head is down and its tail is between its back legs, it is afraid or ashamed. And if it is curious about something, its ears and tail will stick straight up.

Dogs communicate with sounds, too. They bark, growl, howl, and whimper. Other dogs know what their fellow furballs are "saying," and, after a while, so do their owners.

12

Wild Cousins
The wild ancestors of dogs were hunters who traveled in packs. Some that are still around today are:

Wolf	Jackal	Dingo
Fox	African wild dog	Arctic fox

Scientists who have studied cats agree that they purr on purpose. It's one way they communicate. Your cat wants to let you know something—probably that it's happy, according to most scientists. Others have found that cats sometimes purr for different reasons, such as fear or for attention.

How a cat makes that purring sound is a point on which experts don't agree. Some say purring is caused by a vibration in the cat's larynx, located in its throat. Other experts say the sound is made when blood passes through a large vein in the cat's chest.

Even though the domestic cat's ancestors date back over 50 million years, there is still plenty that humans find mysterious about this popular, purring pet.

Why do cats purr?

They aren't revving their engines.

PURRRRRRR

SARDINES

EXTRA

Most cats sleep 16 to 18 hours each day. That includes short periods of rest, called "cat naps."

Having a Happy Cat
A recent Gallup Poll of pet owners found:

90 percent talk to their pets

62 percent give pets Christmas gifts

32 percent let pets sleep in their beds

30 percent leave the TV on to keep their pets company

17 percent keep photos of their pets in their wallets

How fast can horses run?

Walk, trot, canter, gallop . . . they can really move!

Horsing Around
Horses travel at different speeds or "gaits."

Walk:	Similar to a human walk
Trot:	Between a walk and a run
Canter:	Faster than a trot; close to a human jog
Gallop:	The fastest speed; a full run

EXTRA

Secretariat, a thoroughbred, holds the record for being the fastest horse to compete in the Kentucky Derby. He competed in 1973 and won with a time of 1 minute 59 seconds.

Although horses are not the fastest mammals, thoroughbred horses are known for their speed and grace. They are often used in racing against fellow thoroughbreds.

The fastest thoroughbred racehorses can gallop (a horse's fastest speed) at nearly 43 miles per hour (70 kph) over short distances. They can gallop even faster if they're not carrying riders, called jockeys. Over longer distances of at least 2 miles (3.2 km), thoroughbreds can move at about 30 miles per hour (48 kph).

Horse breeders seek out the quickest, healthiest horses to be sires (fathers) and dams (mothers). Breeders hope that the offspring will possess, or improve, its parents' talents.

What is the fastest land animal?

This winner is built for speed.

In just 3 seconds, a cheetah can reach speeds of almost 70 miles per hour (113 kph), giving no other animal the chance to outrun it. Compare that to gazelles, which cheetahs hunt: Gazelles run at speeds of about 45 miles per hour (72 kph).

Cheetahs are born to run. They have strong thigh, back, and shoulder muscles. Plus, these speedy cats have grooves on the pads of their feet and long, thick nails, which dig into the dirt, like soccer players wearing cleats.

Cheetahs' backbones act like a spring, arching as they run. When running at top speed, cheetahs stretch their hind legs beyond their outstretched front legs.

EXTRA

Cheetahs are known for quick bursts of speed. When hunting, their average chase covers about 550 feet (168 m) and lasts only 20 seconds.

On the Fast Track

Cheetahs are fast, but some other animals aren't far behind. Here are a few of the quickest:

Pronghorn Antelope	55 miles per hour (89 kph)
Brown hare	45 miles per hour (72 kph)
Horse	43 miles per hour (69 kph)
Greyhound	42 miles per hour (68 kph)

Horses in the wild have to be watchful of predators. Their best defense is to run away. But it takes longer to break into a gallop if they're lying down. That's why most horses sleep on their feet. Domestic horses (horses kept by human beings) are often known to sleep lying down, however. Scientists believe this may be because the horses have learned to trust their environment and don't expect to be bothered.

Whether wild or domestic, sleeping while they stand up is comfortable for horses. They have a system of muscles, tendons, and ligaments in their legs that "lock," allowing their muscles to rest. This system is called the stay apparatus.

All horses sleep for a total of only 2½ hours in a 24-hour period. They doze for 15 minutes and then are awake for 45 minutes. In the wild, this means they are alert and ready to respond if a predator comes near.

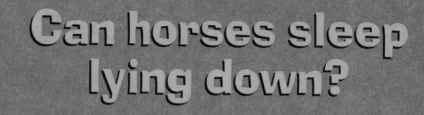

Can horses sleep lying down?

It's against their instincts.

All Four Feet on the Ground
Horses' relatives also sleep standing up. Other members of the horse family are:

Donkey   Mule   Zebra

When winter comes, black bears that live in cold, northern climates snuggle down in their dens for a slumber that may last as long as six months. Their cousins, the grizzlies, also take long winter naps.

This long period of sleep is sometimes called hibernation. But it is actually a "winter sleep." True hibernation means that an animal's heart rate and breathing slow down immensely. The animal enters a state in which it can't be awakened until its body clock says it's the right time. Only a few animals, such as frogs and woodchucks, are true hibernators.

When a bear is in "winter sleep," its vital signs barely decrease, and at the slightest sign of danger, it will wake up. During warm spells, a bear might even leave its den to look for food.

Do bears really sleep all winter?

You don't want to wake a sleeping bear!

EXTRA

During winter sleep, adult males and adolescent bears lose 15 to 30 percent of their weight, while females and newborns lose up to 40 percent of theirs.

What are pinnipeds?

They're mammals that swim, which should give you a clue.

The word pinniped means "fin-footed." Pinnipeds include seals, sea lions, and walruses—all mammals that have "feet" shaped like fins.

Most pinnipeds live in cold regions, such as Antarctica, the Arctic, and the North Atlantic. With layers of blubber to protect them, they don't mind living in the frigid water or resting on the icy shores.

Pinnipeds have great hearing, especially underwater, and they are excellent divers. Seals can hold their breath for up to 7 minutes. Most walruses can cruise underwater for up to 15 minutes!

Although pinnipeds usually travel best in water, they can get around on land, too. They mainly come ashore to rest, mate, and give birth.

EXTRA

Pinnipeds generally give birth to only one baby at a time. This means the pinniped population grows slowly, which is why some species have become endangered.

What do walruses' tusks do?

They're too big for chewing!

EXTRA

Walruses eat mainly clams and other shellfish—up to 6,000 each day! They use their sensitive whiskers to feel for food along the sea floor.

Walruses' tusks are just really big upper teeth. These tusks can reach 3 feet (.9 m) in length. Generally, however, they remain less than 20 inches (50.8 cm) long.

Tusks are mostly used for protection against enemies, such as polar bears. But tusks are also used to help walruses heave their bodies up onto ice floes, or small icebergs. Ice floes can get crowded, so walruses also use their tusks to get more space for themselves. They poke other walruses in order to say, "Hey, make room for me!"

Unfortunately, walruses' tusks have made them a target for hunters, because their tusks are made of ivory. Ivory tusks sell for large amounts of money. For a time, walruses were on the verge of extinction, but new laws have banned the ivory trade. This has helped to save walruses and other animals with tusks.

19

Whales slap their tails and fins, leap up out of the water, and enter again with a resounding splash. Are they playing when they leap? The answer is that no one knows for certain.

Marine biologists who specialize in the study of the water-dwelling mammals, known as cetaceans, observe whales. These biologists try to figure out exactly what their behavior means. Perhaps the slapping, leaping, and splashing is a method of communicating—a sort of sign language. Some scientists believe it's part of whale "courtship" behavior—when they're looking for mates. Others think that the leaping may be a sign that the whales are just having a good time. Scientists continue to study whales, hoping to learn more about these amazing animals.

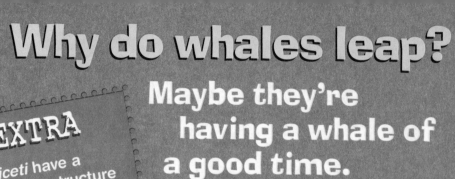

Why do whales leap?

Maybe they're having a whale of a good time.

EXTRA

Mysticeti have a screen-like structure (called baleen) in their mouths, which they use to strain food out of the water. *Odontoceti* use their teeth to capture prey.

Cetaceans alive today are divided into two categories:

Mysticeti (whales with baleen): Gray, right, rorqual, humpback, minke, and blue whales

Odontoceti (whales with teeth): Orca, sperm, bottle-nosed, beaked, killer, beluga and pilot whales; dolphins; porpoises; and narwhals

In a bullfight, a bullfighter, or matador, waves a red cape in front of a big bull—and the bull lowers his horn and charges! But it isn't the color that makes the bull mad. It's the movement of the flapping cloth. In fact, bulls are color-blind, so they see only shades of gray. The cloth is red so that the spectators can see it easily.

Bulls used in bullfighting are specially bred for the sport. They have short tempers and interpret the cape the matador shakes as a taunt, or a tease. The bulls charge because they don't like being teased.

Bullfighting takes place primarily in southern France, Mexico, Portugal, and Spain.

Why do bulls charge at red cloth?

It isn't because they "see red."

EXTRA

The general word for any bullfighter is *torero*. The star bullfighter is the matador. He or she generally has five assistants: three banderilleros on foot and two picadores on horseback.

CHINA SALE!

BULL CARD

21

Why do beavers build dams?

It's a deep secret.

Beaver Enemies

Beavers are so good at building and adjusting dams that the huge rodents are often called "nature's engineers."

Beavers live in freshwater streams, rivers, lakes, and ponds. They build large homes called lodges in the middle of the water or burrow into the banks along the edge of the water. Wherever beavers build, the entrances to their homes are underwater to keep out predators.

Dams, made from trees beavers have cut down, allow the water from incoming streams to come into the area. Dams also stop the water from leaving. Most importantly, dams keep the water deep enough so that it doesn't freeze solid in winter. So beavers can swim to their underwater entrances all year long.

EXTRA

A beaver can cut down an 8-foot (2.4-m)-tall tree in 5 minutes.

Why do pigs roll in mud?

It isn't to make themselves pretty!

EXTRA

One of the most common problems pigs experience is heat stress. So how do you keep hogs happy? Temperatures between 60 and 70°F (16 and 21°C) and plenty of fresh air lead to pleased porkers.

Famous Porcines
You can read all about them.

Charlotte's Web	by E.B. White
Freddy, the Detective	by Walter Brooks
Babe, the Gallant Pig	by Dick King-Smith

Pigs have a reputation for loving mud. These highly intelligent creatures have found the solution to several problems. Unlike dogs, cows, goats, and horses, which have coats of fur, pigs have very pale skin that can burn in the sun. They also don't come equipped with sweat glands to help keep them cool. By wallowing, laying, and rolling in the mud, pigs stay cool, and the mud prevents the Sun's burning rays from damaging their skin. A coating of mud also offers them protection from stinging and biting insects.

Pigs that are kept as house pets, like miniature and potbellied pigs, don't usually have mud baths to stay cool. Their owners are instructed to keep their homes at certain temperatures and to apply sunscreen to the pig's skin before they go outside!

Why do skunks smell so bad?

Get too close, and they'll make a real stink!

Skunks have a powerful defense to protect themselves from animal and human hunters. Special glands at the base of a skunk's tail hold a yellow-colored fluid called musk. When the skunk senses trouble, it arches its back, lifts its tail, and bends its body into a U-shaped position so that both its head and tail point toward the intruder. Then the skunk squeezes the muscles around the glands and squirts the nasty-smelling musk at the attacker.

A skunk can spray up to 12 feet (3.7 m). The awful stink of the musk can hang around for hours, and the wind can carry the smell as far as 1 mile (1.6 km). So if you see one of these black and white creatures coming toward you, quickly walk away. Don't do anything to scare it!

Cousin Stinky
Skunks are members of the weasel family.
Other family members include:

Polecats	Minks	Fishers	Badgers
Ferrets	Martens	Wolverines	Otters

24

Every dog's nose—even the weakest—is more sensitive than any human's. A dog's nose works so well because of the special way in which it is put together. On the inside of a dog's nose is an arrangement of complicated folds. These folds contain many olfactory receptors. The receptors pick up faint traces of chemicals, which the dog's brain interprets as smells. No human being could possibly detect these smells so well!

Dogs gain most of their information about the world around them through their noses. And because their ability to smell comes so naturally to them, humans can often train dogs to "sniff" for particular things in just a few training sessions!

Is a dog's sense of smell better than a human's?

Fido's nose knows. . .

EXTRA

Certain dogs can tell when a fire was set on purpose. They detect the chemicals used to start it. These "arson dogs" can sometimes even identify the people responsible for setting a fire by smelling the same flammable chemicals on their clothing.

25

Why do cats have whiskers?

It's a sensitive issue.

Seeing in the Dark
Cats are great night-stalkers because:

- They have larger retinas (membranes in the eyes that sense light) than humans that let in more light when it is scarce.

- A mirror-like tissue behind each retina makes their eyes glow at night and helps them see better.

- Cats can turn their ears toward a sound, allowing them to rapidly pinpoint the sound's source.

When you can't see in the dark, you put your hands out ahead of you. A cat uses its whiskers for the same purpose, to sense objects it might trip over or bump into. This is the reason why cats can always move quickly and confidently, even in total darkness.

Cats have four rows of whiskers on their muzzle. They also have whiskers on their cheeks and above their eyes. Whiskers are stiffer and much longer than ordinary cat fur. Cats' whiskers also have more nerves, which make them very sensitive to movement and touch. Cats can change the position of these "antennae," fanning them out and forward when walking, and pressing them back and flat against their cheeks when sniffing or biting.

Cat's whiskers don't stop growing. As cats get bigger, their whiskers grow longer. So cats always know when they're into tight squeezes!

Why do elephants have big ears?

Elephants need to keep their cool.

EXTRA

The African elephant is considered a threatened species. The Asian elephant is on the endangered species list.

African elephants live in the savanna, a hot, dry place with only a few trees to provide shade. Flapping their large ears is one way the elephants get relief from the sweltering heat. The motion cools the blood in their ears, which cools their whole bodies. Asian elephants also use their ears to cool themselves, but their ears are smaller. The climate in Asian countries is slightly cooler, and there's also more shade.

Both African and Asian elephants also use their ears to flap away pesky insects and to communicate. By raising, lowering, or bringing their ears forward or back, they can express anger, curiosity, or contentment.

Elephants have other ways of keeping cool. They drink lots of water—up to 18 gallons (81.8 l) each day—and will spend several hours in water, when possible. They also use their long trunks to spray water over their bodies.

27

There are many kinds of foxes, found all over the world. The most common species is the red fox, *Vulpes vulpes*. Not all red foxes are red, though—their fur color can be black or silver. Red foxes are most commonly found in areas where there is a mix of farmland and woodland. Red foxes live throughout Europe, temperate Asia, northern Africa, Canada, and the United States.

Foxes usually make their homes in dens. When the time is drawing near for the female fox (called a vixen) to have her pups, a pair will usually dig a burrow under a tree, or find one that has been abandoned by another animal. Foxes are also known to live in caves and other similarly sheltered places.

Where do foxes live?

They're certainly not pampered pups!

EXTRA

Although foxes belong to the same family (*Canidae*) as dogs and wolves, they share many traits (such as good balance and night vision) with cats. Both cats and foxes evolved in and adapted to similar habitats. They faced many of the same predators and ate much of the same foods. This process is called convergent evolution.

Lemurs are some of the most unusual primates you'll ever see. They're related to apes and chimpanzees, but they're part of a suborder called prosimians, or "before apes." They don't look like apes and chimps at all.

A lemur's nose is pointed, like a fox's, and surrounded by sensitive whiskers. Its eyes seem huge in relation to the size of its head, and its ears are slightly pointed.

Lemurs usually have long tails, and their fur is very soft. They eat fruit, leaves and flowers. Lemurs live in large groups, climbing trees or scampering around on the ground.

These unusual animals live in an unusual place—the island of Madagascar, off the eastern coast of Africa. As far as zoologists know, it's the only place where lemurs live in the wild.

EXTRA

Beneath a lemur's front legs are scent glands that give off a distinct odor. A lemur marks its territory by rubbing its legs against things in the area. Some lemurs use these scent glands to shoot "stink bombs" at other lemurs who threaten to move into their territory.

Where do lemurs live?

Pack your bags, and head to East Africa.

29

Marsupials are mammals that carry their young in pouches. Most marsupials, such as the kangaroo, koala, wombat, numbat, bandicoot, marsupial mole, and marsupial mouse, live in Australia or New Guinea.

Most female mammals develop an organ called a placenta, which is a kind of food supply for their babies. As the baby grows inside its mother, it is nourished by the placenta. But marsupials don't develop placentas. So marsupial babies must be fed outside their mother's body.

When a marsupial baby is born, it's blind, hairless, and completely helpless. So, the marsupial baby crawls up its mother's belly and into her pouch. Tucked inside the pouch, the baby is warm and safe. It feeds on her milk and continues to grow. Several months later, the baby is fully developed and ready to leave the pouch and face the world.

What are marsupials?

The moms of these mammals have a built-in baby seat.

All female kangaroos have one pouch. It's where they carry and feed their young until each baby can survive on its own. A baby kangaroo, called a joey, is born after only one month in its mother's womb. At birth, a joey is about 1 inch (2.5 cm) long, blind, red, and hairless. Once a joey finds its way from the birth opening into its mother's pouch, it remains in the pouch, drinking milk from its mother.

At about six months old, the joey may leave the pouch for a while, but it always returns to be safe, for a meal, or to take a nap. When it is about one and a half years old, the joey permanently leaves the pouch.

Why do kangaroos have pouches?
For little joey, it's home, sweet home.

Why are giant pandas so rare?

They're losing the competition.

Giant pandas are very special animals. But today there are fewer than 1,500 giant pandas left in the wild. The main reason is the pandas' diet. Giant pandas feed mainly on bamboo shoots. They spend about 12 hours a day eating. And they need about 17.5 pounds (8 kg) of bamboo each day.

But too many people pose a threat to the pandas. China, the only place where giant pandas live in the wild, has a growing population of over 1 billion people. This puts humans and pandas in competition for the same land and natural resources. The raising of livestock, such as cattle and sheep, and the clearing of the bamboo forests have damaged about 30 percent of panda-friendly forests.

But there is some good news. The Chinese government has established several panda reserves. Other countries, including the United States, are trying to raise giant pandas in zoos.

What is an okapi?

It's a giraffe's quiet cousin.

EXTRA

Zoologists estimate that there are about 30,000 okapis living in the wild.

Deep in the dense rainforests of Africa's Zaire, the shy, quiet okapi wanders out at dusk to nibble leaves from the trees. It uses its 1-foot (30-cm)-long blue-black tongue to slurp in a branch and pluck off the leaves and tender twigs. Then it slowly wanders off to hide in the shelter of the trees.

Because the okapi lives such a quiet life in such a remote area, zoologists had never even seen one until 1900! Yet once they spotted an okapi, they knew they had found a rare and beautiful animal.

Biologically, okapis are related to giraffes, but okapi's don't really look like them. Okapis grow to be only about 6 feet (1.8 m) tall, and their bodies resemble zebras'. Most of an okapi's body is a dark reddish brown, but its legs have black-and-white stripes all the way up.

The tradition that has become Groundhog Day in the United States originated in Germany in the 1500s. There, farmers watched for badgers to come out from winter hibernation. Farmers believed that if the badger saw its shadow and scurried back into its hole, it meant there would be six more weeks of winter. The farmers took this to mean that they shouldn't plant their fields yet. But if the badger didn't see its shadow, farmers thought spring was coming soon.

When German immigrants arrived in Pennsylvania in the 19th century, they didn't find any badgers. Instead, they relied on the groundhog to predict the change of season.

The tradition continues. Every year on February 2, Americans await the news of whether or not the groundhog has emerged from its den.

34

Can groundhogs predict the weather?

The reality behind this rodent rumor may surprise you.

EXTRA

According to varying records (some kept over a 60-year period), groundhogs' weather "predictions" aren't all that reliable. They've been "right" only 28 to 39 percent of the time.

WEATHER FORECAST Feb. 2

70% CHANCE OF EARLY SPRING

10% CHANCE OF GEESE

Nearly every mammal mother carries her young inside her body until it's ready to be born. But not the platypus and the echidna. These two mammals, both found in Australia, lay eggs instead. The platypus and the echidna are special kinds of mammals called monotremes. They're the only two types of monotremes in the world.

The platypus has a leathery bill, webbed feet, and a flat tail, like a beaver's. The female platypus digs a long burrow, blocks herself in with mud, and lays one or two small, round eggs. She then wraps herself around the eggs to keep them warm until they hatch.

The echidna, also called the spiny anteater, has an anteater-like snout but also has quills, like the porcupine's. During mating season, the female echnida develops a pouch on her belly. She lays an egg and transfers it into this pouch until it hatches.

EXTRA

What makes a mammal a mammal? Scientists look at many traits when they classify animals, but two are essential: Mammals make milk to feed their young, and they have hair or fur.

Do mammals lay eggs?

Two of nature's oddities do!

Straight Versus Curved

There are two types of echidnas—the straight-beaked echidna and the curved-beaked echidna.

Do anteaters eat only ants?

Their dinner menu doesn't have much variety.

The anteater's tube-like snout and long, sticky tongue are specially adapted for only two types of food: ants and termites. Found in South America and Central America, the anteater uses its long, strong claws to rip open the hill-like nests of its preferred prey. Then it pokes its tongue into the wreckage, and gluey saliva picks up the insects.

In the process, the anteater gets a mouthful of dirt, sticks, and gravel, but it swallows everything whole. The anteater's stomach is able to handle anything it eats.

A solitary animal, the anteater only meets up with others of its species to mate. When a baby is born, it climbs onto its mother's back and stays there (except when it's nursing) for three months.

EXTRA

The anteater's nearest relatives are the sloth and the armadillo.

PICKLED ANTS
BBQ ANTS
SWEET & SOUR ANTS
CAJUN ANTS

Biggest and Smallest

Species	Length	Weight
Giant anteater	6 feet (1.8 m)	110 pounds (50 kg)
Silky anteater(.45 kg)	13 inches (34 cm)	1 pound

What is the slowest mammal?

It's a couch potato without a couch!

EXTRA

Sloths almost never visit the ground, but when they do their hair looks like it's standing on end.

Counting Toes

There are two sloth species: the three-toed sloth and the two-toed sloth.

The sloth is especially good at doing nothing. This animal spends day after day just hanging around—literally! Its hands and feet are curved into hooks with claws at the end. The claws allow the sloth to hang upside down from tree branches. Every once in a while, the sloth will nibble at leaves or fruit on the branches around it. Other than that, the sloth doesn't move much.

Because it spends most of its time hanging upside down, the sloth's fur actually grows upside down. This lets rain water wash smoothly off the sloth's coat while it hangs from the branch. In the moist South American forests where it lives, the sloth remains so still that it often becomes covered with algae, turning its fur green!

The Tasmanian devil has earned its name. This meat-eating marsupial is a true terror. It hunts at night and will eat just about anything it finds, from small mammals, reptiles, and birds to the bodies of dead sheep and cows.

European settlers on the island of Tasmania heard the animal's shrieks in the middle of the night and felt for sure that they were in the presence of a demon. That's how the "devil" got its name.

A Tasmanian devil is only about the size of a small dog, but it's much more dangerous. It will attack its prey with sharp teeth and powerful jaws, ripping it apart and eating every last bit—including bones and fur. During the day, the Tasmanian devil will hide in dark, protected places, like hollow logs or rock crevices.

Is there really a Tasmanian devil?

It's a creature from down under.

Devil's Habitat

Tasmania is an island off the southern coast of Australia. It's part of the nation of Australia, and the only place on Earth that you'll find Tasmanian devils in the wild.

Numbats are mammals from Australia, and like many animals from "down under," they're unusual creatures. In spite of their name, numbats aren't related to bats. They look like gray and white striped squirrels with long, pointed snouts. Numbats live in forests, especially in places where there are many fallen trees and rotting logs. That's where numbats find their food.

Termites feed on this decaying wood, and numbats feed on termites. Some people call numbats "banded anteaters," but numbats don't seem to like the taste of ants. For numbats, it's termites or nothing at all. In fact, one numbat can eat as many as 7 million termites a year!

A numbat sticks out its tongue and laps up as many termites as it can. Then it crunches them with its sharp teeth and laps up another bunch.

What do numbats eat?

If you're a termite, run for cover!

EXTRA

Numbats nest in hollow logs on the forest floor. They usually live alone, spending most of the day hunting for termites or relaxing in the sun.

39

What is the difference between a hare and a rabbit?

It's relatively difficult to tell them apart.

Here's the Tricky Part

The animal we know as a jackrabbit is really a hare. It lives in the southwestern United States and northern Mexico. And it can move! Jackrabbits have been known to run 50 miles per hour (80 kph)—almost as fast as cars on the highway.

40

Hares and rabbits are close relatives. It's easier to tell them apart when they're babies. Hares are born with hair. (That's easy to remember!) Their eyes are open, and within a few minutes of birth, they're hopping around and ready to go. Rabbits, though, are born completely helpless. They're bald and blind, and they depend on their mothers to protect and feed them, and to keep them warm.

Usually adult hares are larger and leaner than rabbits. Hares' legs are long, slim, and very powerful. They live in the underbrush, and they don't mind being alone. On the other hand, rabbits are a bit chubbier than hares, and their heads may be slightly more round. They live underground in burrows, called warrens. Rabbits prefer hanging out in groups.

Why does a rabbit wiggle its nose?

The nose knows what a bunny's thinking.

RABBITS KEEP OUT

CARROT

PEAS

UCE

Sensitive Signals
They can't talk, but bunnies have ways of showing their feelings.

Action	Message
Teeth grinding	Calm and content
Stomping	Scared or mad
Grunts	Angry
Hopping a lot	Joy

You probably think it's cute when a furry rabbit wiggles its little nose. But all that wiggling has a purpose. Contrary to popular belief, a rabbit doesn't move its nose to smell things. Instead, the movement shows how the animal is feeling.

A calm rabbit moves its nose slowly. But as a rabbit becomes more interested or upset, it wiggles its nose faster. For example, if you were quietly sitting near a bunny and then quickly moved away, the rabbit's nose would probably wiggle quickly because it's wondering what you are doing. However, if you ran toward the bunny and frightened it, the rabbit would stop wiggling its nose and would immediately dash away.

The desert is a hot, dry place where only a few plants grow. Desert animals, such as camels, often have to go several days without food.

But a camel carries around a handy survival tool: its hump. A camel's hump is made of fat, which comes from the food a camel eats. The fat is stored in the hump until the camel needs it for energy. As the energy is used, the hump becomes smaller until it loses its shape and sags to one side.

A camel's hump serves another purpose: cooling. The hump forms a thick barrier between the camel's heart and other internal organs and the baking rays of the desert sun.

Why do camels have humps?

They aren't portable water coolers, but camels need them to survive.

EXTRA

There are two kinds of camels: the one-humped Arabian camel of North Africa and the Middle East, and the two-humped Bactrian camel of central Asia. Both have long legs and soft, two-toed, webbed feet that let them walk easily over deserts.

Desert Dwellers' Survival Secrets

Toads:	Hide in a hole in the ground until cool night falls
Lizards:	Store fat in their tails
Rabbits:	Huge ears let out body heat
Cactuses:	Spines help prevent water loss and protect cactuses from being eaten

QUESTIONS KIDS ASK ABOUT MAMMALS BIG & SMALL

algae [AL-jee] a group of water plants, such as seaweed

baleen [buh-LEEN] the screen-like structure in the mouth of some whales, instead of teeth; used to strain food from water

blubber [BLUH-buhr] the fat of whales and other large marine animals

camouflage [KA-muh-flozh] the process some animals use to blend in with their surroundings, such as changing the color or pattern of their coat

cetaceans [si-TAY-shuhnz] an order of marine animals, such as whales, dolphins, and porpoises

cones [kohns] the parts of an eyeball that sense color; in humans, three colors of cones sense the three colors of light (red, green, and blue) to provide color vision

convergent evolution [kuhn-VUHR-juhnt e-vuh-LOO-shuhn] the process by which different animals that live in the same places, or environments, gradually change and develop similar traits, such as whales and sharks gradually developing similar torpedo-like body shapes to glide through water quickly

dam [dam] mother of some domestic animals, such as horses; a structure, such as the kind built by beavers, that stops the flow of water

detect [di-TEKT] to find out or discover

diurnal [deye-UHR-nuhl] animals animals that are busy, or active, during the day

domestic [duh-MES-tik] animals animals that are used to living with people, such as cats, dogs, and horses

endangered species [in-DAYN-juhrd SPEE-sheez] animals that are in danger of dying out, or becoming extinct

evolve [e-VOLV] to change or adapt

habitat [HA-buh-tat] the place where an animal or plant normally lives

hibernation [heye-buhr-NA-shuhn] when an animal's heart rate and breathing slow down for a period of time so that the animal can survive difficult conditions, such as an extremely cold winter

ice floes [eyes flohz] a piece of floating ice in the ocean; a small iceberg

immigrant [I-mi-gruhnt] someone who comes to live in a new country

jockey [JO-kee] a person who rides a horse in races

krill [kril] very tiny, shrimp-like animals that live in the ocean

larynx [LAR-ingks] the upper part of the windpipe (air passageway in the throat) where sound is produced

ligaments [LI-guh-muhnts] the tissues in animals' bodies that support organs or the tough tissues in animals' bodies that unite bones or form joints

mammal [MA-muhl] a class of animals, including humans, with hair or fur, in which mothers feed their young with milk produced in their bodies

marsupial [mor-SOO-pee-uhl] an order of mammals of which the females have a pouch where they carry and feed their young

monotreme [MO-nuh-treem] an order of egg-laying mammals, including only the platypus and the echidna

musk [muhsk] a substance that some animals squirt from their bodies to scare away other animals

muzzle [MUH-zuhl] an animal's snout

nocturnal [nok-TUHR-nuhl] animals animals that are busy, or active, during the night

43

QUESTIONS KIDS ASK ABOUT MAMMALS BIG & SMALL

olfactory receptor [ol-FAK-tuh ree-SEP-tuhr] a part of the nose that helps humans and animals pick up scents

placenta [pluh-SEN-tuh] the body part in female mammals that carries food and oxygen to unborn babies; it also takes away the baby's body wastes

plankton [PLANGK-tuhn] tiny plants and animals that live in the ocean

predator [PRE-duh-tuhr] an animal that hunts other animals

prey [pray] an animal that is hunted by another animal for food

primate [PREYE-mayt] the highest order of mammals, including humans, apes, and monkeys

prosimian [proh-SEYE-mee-un] a primitive suborder of primates, including lemurs

retina [TRET-nuh] the part of the eye that reacts to light

rodent [ROH-duhnt] a kind of mammal, such as beavers, mice, and squirrels, that have gnawing teeth

savannah [suh-VA-nuh] a hot, dry grassland with only a few trees and bushes

sires [seyerz] father of some domestic animals, such as horses

social [SO-shuhl] animals animals that live together in a group

solitary [so-luh-TER-ee] animals animals that live alone

stay apparatus [stay a-puh-RA-tuhs] a combination of muscles, tendons, and ligaments that allows a horse to sleep standing up by "locking" its leg joints

tendons [TEN-duhn] the tissues in animals' bodies that connect muscles to bones

threatened species [THRE-tuhnd SPEE-sheez] animals that are likely to become an endangered species (see endangered species)

vertebrae [VUHR-tuh-bray] the small bones of an animal's neck or a human's backbone

vocal cord [VO-kuhl kord] the part of the larynx that produces sounds in humans and other air-breathing animals

wallow [WO-loh] to take delight in; to roll around in

warren [WOR-uhn] a series of connected underground tunnels where a group of rabbits live

zoologist [zoo-O-luh-jist] a scientist who studies animals

QUESTIONS KIDS ASK ABOUT MAMMALS BIG & SMALL